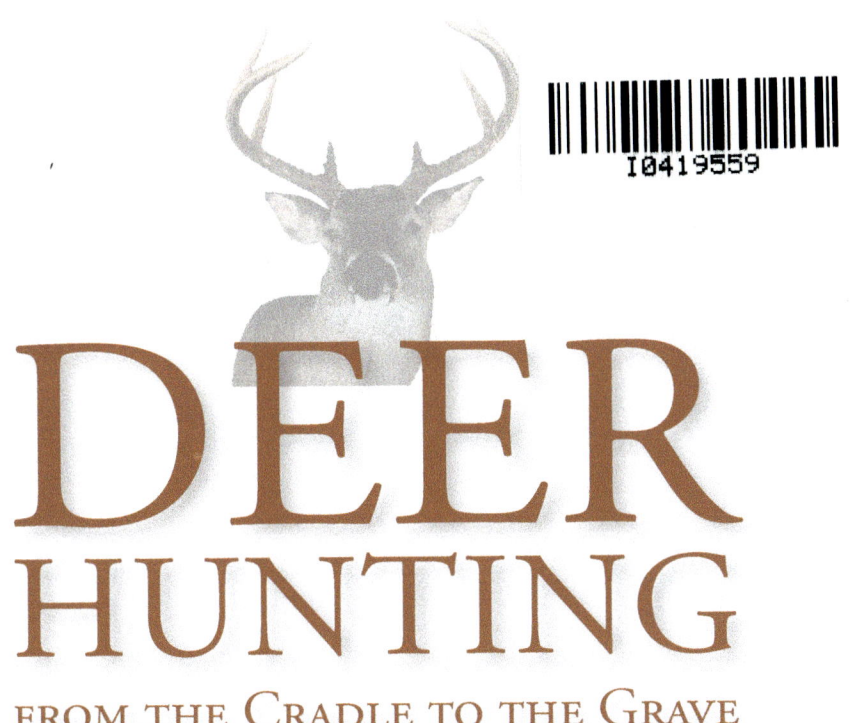

DEER
HUNTING

FROM THE CRADLE TO THE GRAVE

P. R. DORRIS

ISBN 978-1-0980-1072-0 (paperback)
ISBN 978-1-0980-1073-7 (digital)

Christian Faith Publishing, Inc.
832 Park Avenue
Meadville, PA 16335
www.christianfaithpublishing.com

Printed in the United States of America

With affection and appreciation, this book is dedicated to my family, friends, and buddies who were my inspiration and encouragement through a wonderful journey of deer hunting.

C O N T E N T S

INTRODUCTION

The purpose of this book is to relate the ultimate joy that can be derived from all the things that go into becoming a successful deer hunter. This author has spent a lifetime around hunters and hunting and has tried to give valuable information for the beginning or the experienced deer hunter. By observing the wonderful creations of nature and the path trodden by a hunter from the cradle to the grave, it is hoped that you will glean the joy, excitement, and inspiration afforded by deer hunting. The one thing that almost always goes with deer hunting is the cultivation of good friends as you will see in this book. There are so many things in life that one may enjoy, but making good friends like those I have had is worth more than silver or gold. Having spent at least seventy-five years deer hunting in Mississippi and Arkansas, I feel I am prepared to shed a little light on the subject.

CHAPTER 1

Early Years

I was born in 1933 into a fairly unique family with only one brother, but my dad had six brothers who lived near our humble dwelling at a little place called Colby, Mississippi. We may have had fifty residents counting black and white people, but everyone hunted and fished in those days due to poverty conditions, for recreation, and to put food on the table. My dad jokingly said we lived in Plumb Nearly (Plumb out of the city and nearly out of the country). The nearest little town was Holly Bluff, Mississippi, with one grocery store, a gas station, cotton gin, and a soy bean elevator, which my dad managed in later years, after the rise of soybean farming instead of cotton farming in that area. Prior to these jobs, he raised cotton and had a little country store during many years of my life.

Well, to get to the point, all the men in the Dorris family looked forward to the deer season each year more than anything else in their lives. Of course, you can imagine the competition among the hunters, and as a child, I grew up with deer racks attached to all the walls in the house, especially the racks that were noteworthy. These men were all crack shots with any available gun, and you have to know they put plenty of meat on the table from white-tailed deer.

My dad had four guns when I was growing up, and I learned to shoot them all. He kept a .38 Special Smith and Wesson long-barrel revolver pistol under his pillow in case an intruder came into the house, a 12-guage Browning automatic shotgun with which he hunted deer, ducks, squirrels, and quails, and he had a .22 Remington automatic rifle with which he hunted squirrels.

I can remember when I first asked to learn to shoot my dad's shotgun and he let me shoot it, but he warned it would really kick back hard. I also remember how scared I felt pulling the trigger because he was truly right. I was probably about eleven or twelve years old. It kicked the living day lights out of me, but I kept trying and flinching until I lost my fear and got to be a pretty good shot. When I went with my dad deer hunting, we always borrowed my uncle's shotgun for me to shoot. I killed my first deer in the vast stands of hardwood timber with many acorns of different kinds, plus many browse foods. Our main hunting areas were about a fourth of a mile down a dirt path which we travelled on horses.

Even before I was old enough to hunt, I would always ask for cowboy suits, boots, and a cap pistol for Christmas, birthdays, etc. I can remember sleeping in my clothes the night before a deer hunt so that when I heard my dad rise about five o'clock in the morning to go deer hunting, I would always be ready to get on the back of his horse and go with him. We had a little trouble once when I insisted on riding on the front of the saddle. I was led to know very quickly if I insisted on riding in front on the saddle, I would have to stay home.

Another unusual event of my childhood was probably because of the incident that occurred when I wanted to ride Dad's horse on the front instead of the back, as we rode to the hunting grounds. One day, when my dad came home, he had been to the auction and bought me my very first small black horse. I was overcome with joy and knew he was the best dad in the world. There was one problem. I was too short to put my foot in the stirrup of the saddle and get on the horse without assistance, but I was not to be defied by my short stature. We had a small country store at that time which I alluded to earlier. We bought Coca Cola's in big wooden boxes, and I would stack two boxes together on the store porch to make myself tall enough to get on my horse. I loved that little horse, and I had just gotten into the woods on him when I killed my first deer. When Dad returned from his favorite deer stand, he was shocked, surprised, and happy. We were both so happy he had bought me a horse, and I had killed my first deer.

Thinking back on so many memorable things which happened in my early years of deer hunting, I will have to tell you another really big incident in my young life. One day, a friend of my dad's drove up from a city about fifty miles to deer hunt with him. He had a beautiful red horse with a white blazed face in his trailer. I was still in middle school. I couldn't go that day for some reason. Well, they came riding in after the hunt, and the man was a fairly wealthy man who had brought his wife's fine horse.

The horse was beautiful but not a real big horse. He said, in an angry voice, "Would you like to have this horse?" He said, again in a loud voice, "Would you like to have this horse?" I could not believe what he asked! He then said disgustedly and in a loud voice, "This horse really acted wild and crazy when I was in the woods, but my wife never had trouble with him."

I immediately said, "Yes, sir, I would love to have him."

I was totally startled when he actually said, "Well, he is yours."

Dad had seen the horse wildly "acting up" in the woods and had some misgivings about me having the horse, but he agreed to let me have the horse. He was a gorgeous horse and much larger and more beautiful than my little black gentle horse.

I will relate a few early episodes after I got him and before he became the "perfect horse." The first time I rode him, I was about a half a mile from home, ready to go back to our house, and he started running and didn't stop until he got back to our house. He would turn in to our driveway so swiftly he would nearly throw me off. There was no way I could stop this bad habit for a while. I guess he was just looking for a familiar place. One thing I learned very soon was that he was the fastest running horse I had ever seen, so I started daring my black and white friends to race with me. (Riding horses was one of the favorite pleasures of my high school friends.) He brought me great joy, but for a long time, he continually turned into our house so fast when he got home that I really had to hold on tight to keep from falling off. One other bad habit was that he would allow no one to ride him except me.

Once, a black man who lived close by came to our house and asked my dad if he could borrow my horse. My Dad said, "Yes!" John Wall tried and tried to get on the horse, but he couldn't keep the horse still enough to get on.

He said to my dad, "No, sir, Mr. Dorris, I don't believe I want to ride this horse."

I think only the wife of the man who gave him to me must have ever ridden him. My size and weight were probably the only reason he ever accepted me.

Now, as I look back to the age at which I killed my first deer, I can tell you that mode of hunting has changed dramatically, with the use of fancy automated corn feeders and game cameras also on every tree. My friends often boast of their children killing deer at age seven, eight, and so forth. I realize that people who work don't have much time to stay in the woods, and corn and cameras can certainly be enticing, but I got so old without that mode of hunting I just decided to stay with the old more difficult and time-consuming method of looking for deer trails, rubs on trees and bushes, scrapes on the ground, shed antlers, acorns, and other food and water sources. That method had always paid off for my father's generation and now for my generation. I would like to say that over all these years, I have killed, in Mississippi and Arkansas, about as many deer and as big deer hunting with the old methods as those who have used the newer methods. The old method is also the cheapest. It seems that the newer deer hunting methods have become common to the deer and that they have also enticed many wild hogs into Arkansas and other states. The hogs have become a real problem in some areas hanging around the deer feeders, eating the corn, and also rooting up farm crops causing great destruction. The deer also seem to have gotten somewhat wise to what is going on with this new hunting method, and it can also be costly.

So many changes have come about since I first started hunting. Different bows, muzzleloaders, and modern guns are fantastic. There are straight bows, compound bows, crossbows, and others, and there are also very modern powerful and accurate guns. There are also various kinds of stands like ground stands—sitting in a camouflaged chair, rotating stools—a camouflaged canvas house-like stand, above ground stands like climbing tree stands, metal ladder tree stands, and box tree stands, and yet, in the old days, I have killed many deer just sitting on the ground by a tree or just sitting on a log or a fallen tree.

I remember an unusual event that occurred when I was hunting with my dad and his hunting club. They ran dogs, and about 11:00 a.m., they stopped hunting, and went to the camp for lunch (they always had a cook, and many spent the night at the camp, but my dad always wanted to sleep in his own bed at night instead of the "roughing it" beds which most men used when staying overnight). Well, I was still sitting quietly on my log, and I heard some dogs really running deer, and the buck and doe stopped right in front of me. The buck was right in front of my log, and the doe came right up on his other side and stopped abruptly. They were listening for the dogs that had not caught up with them yet but were on their trail. I had a powerful rifle that day (forgot whose I was using), but I shot the buck, and that bullet went right through the buck and killed the doe too. You're talking about somebody who was surprised! It took me a few moments to realize what had happened. Those powerful rifles are unbelievable!

One thing I learned in my early years was that the school had a rule that you could not play in a ball game if you missed a class the day of the game. You have to realize that my Holly Bluff, Mississippi, Consolidated School had only about 250 students from the first through the twelfth grade, and every player was needed to have a complete team. My dad and brother were going to take our liver spotted pointer bird dog for a quail hunt, and I didn't tell them I had a basketball game that night. I finally prevailed upon my dad to let me go quail hunting. Well, he did, and I didn't get to play basketball that night either. I guess it was worth missing, despite the fact that I did love basketball, but the pie was even sweeter because I killed more quail than either my brother or dad (which was quite unusual).

One of the saddest days of my life was when I went off to college and knew I would have to get rid of my horse because I would not be able to keep him and I never knew how often I would be able to come home and hunt, but I did come home every weekend that I could, and I never lost the desire through all those early years to deer hunt as often as I could.

Now, let's get ready to think about deer hunting: When one goes deer hunting, it is always a good thing to have several things in your pocket or in a bag, fanny pack, etc. I would first have on a hunting suit of the "scent lock" type. The suits have a layer of charcoal between the two layers of cloth. They were devised during war so that no human odor could escape from the material and warn enemies. Of course, I could only afford one after I started teaching because they are a little pricey, about $300, but worth every cent (although not absolutely required, just make sure you are clean and emit as few odors as possible). Since a deer's most valuable asset to avoid danger is his nose, I wanted to eliminate odor as the first thing so I could expect the deer never to smell my scent and most of the time they would come in very close range. I have had many deer to walk right up to or under my stand and never smell me. Generally, they can smell human scent from a pretty good distance, but the way the wind is blowing has much to do with the distance. There are also sprays that can block smell when sprayed on clothing.

If you hunt, do it early in the morning and late in the afternoon, and every hunter knows early morning and late afternoon are the best times to hunt deer because they rise early from their beds and start feeding. About midday, they go back to their beds and get up from the beds to feed again late in the afternoon. Therefore, a good flashlight, deer caller, pocket knife, whistle, warm gloves, orange tape to mark trails in the woods, hand and foot warmers, compass, face mask, rope, cell phone, binoculars, first aid kit, and pistol (when bow or muzzleloader hunting especially, since you will probably have only one shot) are really important, and when you are leaving your stand, especially after late afternoon hunting, you never know when you will run into a bear, a group of coyotes, unsavory characters, etc.

High School Teaching Years and Hunting

The first year I attended college, I went to Holmes Junior College in Goodman, Mississippi, and in the second year, I transferred to Mississippi College in Clinton, Mississippi, where I finally earned my BS teaching degree in biology. I did, however, have a little interlude which I will explain later before completing my BS degree (chapter 3). After receiving my BS degree, I was in need of a job and some income, so I went to a teacher fair where high school superintendents came to find terminal degree teachers to teach. When I met with the high school superintendents, a man named Mr. Ladd was looking for a science teacher and asked me to come to Wilmot, Arkansas, to teach. I said to him, "Well, I was looking for a school in Louisiana because on the automobile tags, a sign read: 'The hunting and fishing paradise of the world'."

He quickly said, "Well, Wilmot is only four miles from the Louisiana line." He also said, "Wilmot has one of the highest paying salaries in the district." Then he added, "We have Lake Enterprise that runs right through the town, and we have wonderful hunting grounds."

I perked up my ears and thought this might be just as good state and location as Louisiana for deer hunting and all my other desires for hunting and fishing. After taking the job, I realized that ten minutes after school was over; I could be on Lake Enterprise fishing, setting out trot lines, duck hunting, etc. The deer hunting was also great because in that flat delta land (just like the place I grew up), there were massive stands of hardwood and pine timber with ideal food, water, and protection for deer. Quail hunting, dove hunting, duck hunting, squirrel hunting, and deer hunting were wonderful, and I had the time of my life living in that small town with a population of about five hundred people. The teaching was great because I had wonderful little country students, grades seven to twelve, who also loved to hunt and fish with me.

I was only a little over one hundred miles from my hometown in Holly Bluff, Mississippi, so on many weekends and holidays, I crossed back over the mighty Mississippi River and went back to my old Holly Bluff hunting and stomping grounds. No matter where I was, I could always make time for deer hunting, and to go home and hunt with my dad was always a treat. My brother had moved away by this time, and we no longer had good hunts as a trio.

CHAPTER 3

A Surprise Interlude

When I had ninety hours credit at Mississippi College (it took 124 to graduate), I decided to apply to medical school. That was in the early 1950s, and it was very hard to be accepted into medical school. Well, it was almost miraculous that I was accepted into the University of Mississippi Medical School. Now, the one thing I had not planned on was that going to medical school was a very expensive endeavor. We had no money, but my mother had one brother who had some money, so we asked him for a loan, and he said, "Well, I do have a little money, but my wife and I are old and may need it in our last years," so we could not get money from him for me to attend medical school. It was kind of ironic in the end because his wife died, and he ended up living in our house until he died. Well, aside from that, we tried the bank for a loan next in Yazoo City, Mississippi. Those were lean years, and it was hard to get a big loan in those days from any bank, and we had very little collateral to put up. Today, if one is accepted into medical school, almost any bank will let them borrow money.

There is one other fact which I will divulge at the end of this book that will surprise you greatly. Anyway, my dad had an old 1935 Ford car which he sold, and my family boarded school teachers so they had a little money to get me started and, hallelujah, an organization sprung up overnight called the Mississippi Medical Foundation. This was the deal: They would give money for medical school if the student would sign a paper saying they would come back to rural areas in Mississippi and practice medicine for five years and the loan would not have to be repaid. That is exactly what I would have wanted to do anyway.

Talking about someone as happy as a Lark, I got going pretty well into the second semester of that first year the Mississippi Medical Foundation appeared and very soon they "flew by night," just vanished as abruptly as they had appeared. (See chapter 2, High School Teaching)

I only lacked thirty-four hours to finish my BS degree when I was accepted to medical school so I went back to Mississippi College, finished my BS degree, and that is how I got to Wilmot, Arkansas, to teach, and this would be my first teaching job in Arkansas.

CHAPTER 4

Back to the Teaching Arena and Hunting

After a tenure of four years science teaching at Wilmot, Arkansas, and a brief interlude to medical school, I started applying for scholarships to graduate school. I was accepted to graduate school, and the scholarship was sufficient for each semester. I was now going to work on a master's degree (MS) and then a doctor of philosophy (PhD). This took about five to six years, but I had always loved my high school teaching so much that I knew that teaching must be my calling.

Don't ever believe that this higher education prevented me from deer hunting and all other kinds of hunting and fishing. Wherever I seemed to be, I would always find a fertile field for hunting everything I could on weekends, holidays, etc. One advantage at the University of Mississippi where I attended graduate school was that there was a big reservoir very close to the university, and my major professor and advisor loved goose hunting, so I had some weekends in which I participated in goose, duck, and deer hunting, but in my heart, I knew there was nothing that "turned me on" and gave me the excitement of deer hunting. I also did some quail hunting with my advisor and another husband and wife team.

Finally, after about five years, I had my advanced degrees and was ready to go into college teaching. Mr. Ladd, the Wilmot High School superintendent, knew Dr. Russel, the president of Henderson

State University, and what I am about to tell you is pretty astounding: Mr. Ladd knew that President Russel was looking for a professor of biology, and he told President Russell I had left Wilmot to get advanced degrees in science and he might want to contact me. Well, hallelujah, Henderson State University in Arkadelphia, Arkansas, was only about 140 miles from Wilmot, Arkansas, where I had taught high school for four years. I knew right off that Wilmot had been a "place of beauty and a joy forever," and I knew immediately that I would love to be in similar surroundings and similar "stomping grounds." I knew there would be lovely hunting places that held many deer. To make a long story short, but not really short, because when I get to telling you about only a few of the fantastic deer hunts and wonderful hunting buddies I have had for the last fifty-two years in Arkadelphia, it turns into a great episode. It will make you know that I had found my calling and a hunting and fishing paradise which was and is unfathomable.

Teaching and Chairing the Biology Department

As soon as I finished my doctoral dissertation and course work, I came to Arkadelphia to talk to the chairman of the biology department because I was ready to start a teaching career. The chairman was a stately woman thinking of retiring, and now she was interviewing me as one to teach and one who would later take over her job as chair and do all the jobs which she did. Five years later when she retired, I did become chair of the biology department. At the interview, after she went over all the mandatory requirements and all the things she was doing, and classes I would be teaching, she asked if I thought I would be interested in the position as an Assistant Professor. I knew I was qualified and interested because I would not be so far away from Mississippi where I had grown up, it was not a large community with about ten thousand population, it was not a huge university, the town was small, and the students would be like the ones I grew up with, very country-like, sweet, humble, churchgoing folks much like myself. I learned during my four years at Wilmot that Arkansas was a wonderful place to hunt, fish, and live.

Now, back to the interview with Dr. Adelphia Basford who was looking me squarely in the eye and asking if I thought I would like to teach at Henderson State University. I looked her squarely in the eye and said, "Yes, I would like this job, but there is something you should know about me: I am a hard worker and a dedicated teacher, but, on weekends, I will hunt and fish because they are my favorite pastimes, and I will pursue them in my spare time."

By the time you, the reader, get to the end of this book, you will be very shocked and surprised at why I knew I must be honest and upfront about this decision to tell her who I was and what I would be destined to do in my spare time. She, to my surprise, did not seem opposed to this statement, and I took the job for thirty years—hunting and fishing every chance I got and taking her place as chairman of the department for the last nineteen years of my teaching career at Henderson State University until I retired in 1996.

In these early years, I was making enough money to keep adding to my collection of guns. I already had a 12-gauge Remington automatic shotgun and a .22 caliber Remington automatic rifle, and a .32 caliber Smith and Wesson pistol which I bought the year I graduated from high school and went to work in Jackson, Mississippi, to work as a secretary in the office of the Lt. governor to have a summer job before going to Holmes Jr. College in Goodman, Mississippi, that fall. I also had a little ten-foot aluminum flat bottom boat which I could put in that big trunk of my old well-used Pontiac car. Now, I was not a gun collector for sure, but I did better my collection when I got to Arkadelphia, with a 30-06 Remington automatic rifle, a .38 caliber Smith and Wesson revolver pistol, and a small pocket size 22 revolver pistol made by American Arms Co. I called it my "pocket pistol" and never went to the deer woods (or many other places) without it. I explained earlier why I had it among the items I always carried to the woods. I actually took it with me almost everywhere I went, because it was short, lightweight, and fit into almost any pocket. It offered me protection and was a good little concealed weapon in case of trouble. Fortunately, I never had to use it because of trouble, but it surely did give me a good feeling of confidence in case I needed it. I also bought another 12-gauge Browning automatic shotgun, but I got a more powerful one that was camouflaged, and it could be used for deer, ducks, squirrels, quail, or whatever was in season. I used it mostly for duck hunting, because I always loved the 30-06 rifle best for deer, even though I had learned to hunt with a 12-gauge shotgun during those early years. And, yes, I bought a nice eighteen-foot bass boat with a 115-horsepower Yamaha motor, and when no hunting seasons were opened, I could always go to the big Lake DeGray in Arkadelphia and catch a string of fish (well, almost always).

The years moved on, and through all those wonderful hunting years, one of my two main hunting buddies was destitute, with a mother dying of emphysema (though she never smoked) and a blind father who, in early years, worked for the telephone company, but now he was blind, and my buddy was, from birth, handicapped with a short withered right arm and a very small right hand. Holding a good well-paying job was a real problem, so in order to feed the family, we always tried to kill as many deer as was allowed each year so the family could have delicious and nutritious meals for survival. They also had a garden with which a close neighbor helped. The father had saved a little money over the years, hoping my almost five-foot buddy might go to college, but the father's blindness and inability to work usurped all the available money for even a decent livelihood. Both my first two (number one and number two) hunting buddies had only a high school education, but despite their infirmities, they could build seven- to eight-foot wooden ladder deer stands we hunted on in the early years of my teaching in Arkadelphia. While I was teaching school, and much of the time chairing the biology department, they were squirrel hunting, which opened before deer season opened. All this time, they were looking for good deer signs, good trails, deer rubs on trees, scrapes on the ground, good browse, shed antlers, water and food sources, etc. They needed the meat, and I was certainly the recipient of some great places to hunt and good solid wooden deer stands.

My Biology classes were also fascinating and wonderful. I will share a very unusual occurrence related to deer. One of my biology students brought to school an 8 point beautiful deer with great antlers and no scrotum. I proved to my class, by dissection, that deer, like other animals, may exhibit hermaphroditic characteristics with no scrotal sack containing sperm cells, but only with ovaries instead. Teaching Biology and about all our wonderful creations has truly been my calling.

My First Two Hunting Buddies (Number 1 and Number 2)

The way I met my first two hunting buddies was shortly after I first got to town, and not in the way one might think. Teachers were not paid very high salaries in those early years when I arrived on the scene in Arkadelphia in 1966. I decided I could add to my bank account a little if I got a job delivering papers after school every afternoon. I also knew that money could be used for one of the ten faculty houses which the school rented to new faculty, at a very low price, as a drawing card to get new teachers. It was understood that the faculty houses would have to be vacated after five years, and I would have to find a place to rent, buy, or build. Rental property was very scarce in this town. Therefore, I thought I could save my paper route money for the day I would have to rent, buy, or build a house. I already knew I loved my work, my hunting and fishing, the students, the people in the town, those with whom I worked, and on and on. So after I had been here for five years, I had to find somewhere to live, so I looked for a house to rent but could never find the necessary location that would fit my budget. In 1970, I talked to a contractor, got a loan from the bank, and had a local builder start my home. The house was finished and ready for me to move into in 1971. Believe it or not, I finally got it paid off in a little less than the thirty years, and in 1972, I got into the cattle business and stayed in that business thirty-five years while I was still teaching. I guess I was a real dunce for punishment!

I knew the Daily Siftings Herald office needed more paper carriers, so the first day I went to the pickup place for the newspapers that would be delivered around the town and in the country, I saw many others who were paper carriers waiting, as usual, for their papers too. I met both of my would-be hunting buddies as we spoke of love and passion for deer hunting, and it was very advantageous for me because they had lived in Arkadelphia most of their lives, were about my age, and had many friends and acquaintances who would let us deer hunt on their land.

I felt so fortunate to have two very special hunting buddies through all these years who did not have eight to five jobs as I did. They spent many hours looking for good places to hunt, getting permission to hunt on private lands, and scouting every wonderful place which we would hunt. They also spent many hours building tree stands for the three of us. They used two 2 x 4s for the side pieces and steps of the ladders and a piece of 1/4 to 1/2 inch plywood for the seats. They would cut out a triangle at the back of the plywood that would then fit snugly against the tree. Even this year, as I walked through the woods to my metal store bought sixteen-foot stands, I saw the remains of some of our old wooden stands. I have one metal stand which is within ten feet of one of our old wooden stands, now in pieces on the ground. One of them is the stand that went around the tree and put me on the ground.

CHAPTER 7

The Fall

I was very lucky through all those years I hunted on those primitive wooden stands to not get hurt, but I was always careful because I hunted often by myself. I explained above how we constructed our seven- and eight-foot wooden stands. They were attached to the tree with two ratchet straps.

Well, one day, I was hunting alone, and we always tightened the ratchet straps very tightly around the tree and deer stand. It had come a really gully washer rain the night before my hunt. I had hunted until about 11:00 a.m., and the male deer were in the rut (breeding stage). A big eight-point buck came by chasing a doe, and I killed the buck. After sitting still in my deer stand for a few minutes to see if there would be any more activity, looking at the dead buck on the ground to the left of my stand, I decided to come down from my wooden stand with my 30-06 Remington automatic rifle strapped around my back and shoulder. About the time I got down the first two steps, the stand started slipping and going around the tree so fast that I had to make a big decision to jump or ride the tree stand down. I made a quick decision to ride it down, but it was going so fast around the wet tree, to which it was attached, that it threw me off. My gun was still around my shoulder and back, but I landed on my back, and my head fell right between a tree and a ragged old stump with jagged edges. I was so lucky to not break my back, have a concussion, ruin my gun, or knock the telescopic sight off my rifle (I always had a telescope on my rifle, whether high powered or 22 caliber rifle. I even had a telescope on my bow and muzzleloader.) I did love looking through those scopes, putting the crosshair on my target, and pulling the trigger (smile). My two hunting buddies had gone to Hot Springs, Arkansas (to shop), which was about thirty miles away. Whew! What an experience. I still had to load that buck on my four-wheeler, get out of the woods to my truck, and get home which was about ten miles. I was so lucky! Back in those days, we had no cell phones, but after this incident, I did buy us each a walk-ie-talkie so we could stay in touch when we were all in the woods. Not that a walkie-talkie would have done any good with my buddies thirty miles away in Hot Springs, but after that experience, I really felt a need to be in contact because we all had different deer stands within the same scope of woods. We could now communicate with each other in the woods. (Too bad we had to wait a few years before cell phones arrived on the scene.)

C H A P T E R   8

The Deer Loader

Another invention came on the scene during these years. I saw an advertisement in a Mississippi paper that advertised a mechanical loader that would bolt to the back rack of my newly acquired Yamaha four-wheeler. Before I was financially able to buy a four-wheeler, I had a small two-wheel trail bike, like the ones the Fish and Game Commission had, but it was not very good for hauling big deer, like the ones you will see in this book. I was so happy when I was finally financially able to buy a $3000 four-wheeler and a loader which cost about $300, but they were worth every penny and many times over. There is no telling how many of the 365 deer I killed over the fifty-two years I have hunted here that I loaded with that little simple mechanical loader. This is the way it worked: it had a long stake-like shaft that fit underneath the four-wheeler (when the clip pins that held it up were removed), it would stick in the ground in a vertical position beneath the back of the four-wheeler. One would then back the four-wheeler very slowly, the sliding piece which stuck up at the top would go down very slowly to the ground, lying flat on the ground, the deer could be pulled on to that piece, and by driving the four-wheeler very slowly forward, the loader rack, with deer attached, was now lifted to the back rack of the four-wheeler and the deer could be rolled on to and attached with rubber straps to the back rack for hauling. It is now ready, with deer on four-wheeler, to be hauled to my truck where I will ride up my ramp into the back of my truck or into a small trailer which I sometimes pull behind my truck. After using that loader most of fifty-two years and hauling out three deer this year too, I have to admit its age is showing, as is mine. This will probably be my last year to hunt, since these long-time buddies are dead, in the nursing home, or have left Arkadelphia, but the loader has served me well through three different four-wheelers all these years, and it still works well on my 2001 Yamaha four-wheeler. I am told that the Mississippi loader company is no longer in business and the company label has been worn off my loader, so I wouldn't know where to go looking for one like it now. I do know, however, there are some nice loaders to be found, but they will be pricier now, and they will probably be electric, much nicer and much more expensive.

Skinning a Deer: The Golf Ball Bloodless Method

Hunting Buddies #1 & #2

My first two hunting buddies and I had worked out a miraculous method of dressing deer which we called "the bloodless golf ball method." We worked together in such a harmonious manner that we were to the point we could dress a deer in eight minutes. Seems impossible, doesn't it? Listen very carefully, if you have two hunting buddies, you can do the same thing, and it is almost completely bloodless.

The first thing we would do is tie a rope around the deer's neck, quickly tie the other end to the long hay probe on the front of my tractor, lift the probe up high (see picture), and when the deer was raised off the ground with the hydraulic lift, we would each have a certain position for the dressing job (our hunting knives were kept very sharp). The positions were these: One would cut a ring completely around the neck, leaving only a skin attachment at the back of the neck. One would cut a ring around the upper legs, just above the front feet. One would cut a ring around the lower legs, just above the back feet. The skin would be cut up the inside length of each leg, and then we would make an incision right down the ventral midline (being careful not to cut into the internal viscera). Finally, we would use what we called the golf ball method. We would, with a short piece of rope, tie a golf ball in the neck skin which had been peeled down about twelve inches. I always kept a golf ball in my pickup truck (a rock will work too). Now tie a ten- or twelve-foot rope into the smaller rope tied around the golf ball rope in the neck skin and attach the long rope to a four-wheeler or truck. Drive forward, and the skin will pull right off.

Finally, we would cut the hams and shoulders off and drag the knife down each side of the vertebra to get the tenderloin strip, and that all becomes a very fast operation. With three of us working rapidly, we could complete the dressing operation, and we called it our "eight-minute golf ball bloodless dressing method." Now, all you had to do was take the bloodless carcass, with all the inner parts, still intact, and dispose of it.

In later years, I sometimes got pretty lazy, especially if I killed a deer at dusk, and just carried the deer to the slaughterhouse and dropped it off to have it completely processed by the company. The going rate this year in Arkansas was about $100, and that was cut tenderize steaks, ground pieces into hamburger, and wrapped and frozen in very heavy white paper or vacuum packages. These packages keep air from entering and keep the meat very fresh for a long time. The vacuum packaging is quite an improvement, so always request this type of wrapping if you have a choice. In my last few years, since my buddy (number one) died at age ninety, and buddy (number two), born with the withered arm and tiny hand, has been in the nursing home for the last three years (and, truthfully, they have not been able to hunt with me for the last ten years due to physical problems), I have gotten really lazy and have had the slaughterhouse do the whole job of dressing, cutting, freezing, and wrapping. In the days when I had to make sure we had all tags filled or as many tags as possible to have enough meat for the family of my (buddy number two), we would try to fill all tags, which could have been up to eighteen deer this year. Of course, we didn't need all that venison the last few years due to information in this paragraph. This year (2018), each hunter had six tags. When we first started hunting together in 1966, the deer were scarce, and one could only kill three deer (half the number as now). The deer population has really grown, and only two legal bucks (at least three Tines on one side or be a button buck) can be killed, but one can kill as many as six does or two bucks and four does in Arkansas. Of course, we were not able to fill every tag every year, but my little (number two buddy), who needed the meat for the family livelihood, would never let us stop as long as the family needed meat.

CHAPTER 10

The Cattle Business

One of the teachers in the math department of the university said to me one day, "Since you love animals so much, why don't you let me go to the sale barn and buy a few cows for you?" (Of course, I would pay for them). He said, "I have a young man named Charles who would be glad to help you for a meager fee since he is already helping me." Having never grown up around cows, I knew very little, but I did love all animals, and so I agreed. Mr. Thaxton, the man who made the suggestion, did send the boy some days to help a little, but he finally quit coming. Mr. Thaxton had bought me four black Angus cows, and I had rented a thirty-acre pasture from Mrs. Hasley who worked in the nursing department at Henderson. I had no catching pen, no barn, only a small watering pond which almost dried up every summer. Well, I had no bull with those four cows, so I knew if I was going into the cattle business, I would have to invest in a holding pen with a head gate and build a small barn, which I did, with the aid of one other teacher and one student. When we started summer school, we worked every afternoon (except Sunday) to get that job done. The other teacher had many tools because the father had been a builder. This is just one very good example of great friends who were not even hunters at that time. The student did, however, later become a wonderful hunter.

Now, as a cattle operator, I decided to build my herd with four black Angus cows, but I thought I might like to have an exotic breed. There were already many breeders who had black Angus, Herefords, Charolais, Brangus, etc. in Arkansas, so I decided I would have Simmental cattle from the Simme Valley of Switzerland, but I would need a bull. Since this was an exotic breed, I learned a bull would cost $10,000. I knew a poor schoolteacher who spent too much money on hunting and fishing could never afford such. I knew two other people who had cattle pretty close to my thirty acres, and they told me they were going to Hot Springs(about thirty miles away) in a couple of weeks, on a certain weekend, to take advantage of a school that was being offered to teach people how to perform artificial insemination in cattle. I decided that might be a way I could get some Simmental blood into my four black Angus cows, so I went to the school and bought a nitrogen tank which was necessary to keep viable semen frozen in liquid nitrogen. After being in the cattle business twenty-five years, in 1997, a tornado came through Arkadelphia and killed six people, hung cows in trees, and blew away all my big hay rings, feed troughs, two pole barns, head chutes, catching pens, and my seventeen-foot camper. There were also other untold damages, such as blowing down all trees, fences, etc., around my now 192 acres which I had accumulated over the twenty-five years I had cattle. I knew it was time for me to quit cattle farming because I was now about sixty-five years old and did all my own work with haying, breeding, etc., since I had retired from teaching in 1996. I had already had one knee joint replacement and was awaiting another. It was time for me to retire from a hobby which I had loved, but I had finally achieved my purpose. I now had one hundred heads of registered purebred Simmental cattle, but it took twenty-five years and four generations with use of artificial insemination. My dream had come true! That breed was now highly coveted because they were a much bigger breed than our common breeds of cattle, they were almost disease-free, they had no bad inbred physical problems, and they were docile beautiful red and white or yellow and white animals. Later, cattle operators started using black Simmental semen to get black coloration into the herd.

Well, just before the tornado, I had just bought my first cab tractor with air conditioning, heat, radio, etc. That tornado caused so much anguish to so many, but I was extremely lucky because none of my cows were blown away, and I was able to sell every cow and bull I had right out of the pasture. I never had to carry one to the sale barn. People came to the pasture and bought them like "hot cakes."

The main thing I want the reader to know, however, is I still went deer hunting nearly every weekend and was fortunate that the tornado came in March after the main deer seasons had come and gone from October through December.

I lived for the deer seasons, and since my handicapped hunting buddies helped me with my winter farm work, we still hunted diligently early mornings and late afternoons and killed our limits nearly every deer season. I hunted the early bow season first with a compound bow, and then I got a crossbow because I was old enough. Today, anyone can hunt with a crossbow. I believe sixty-five was the age that people had to be in those years before they were legal. I also hunted with my 30-06 Remington automatic rifle and a black powder Thompson/Center muzzleloader. Today, the Arkansas Game and Fish Commission will allow six deer to be taken, with only two being bucks, as I pointed out earlier. We always managed to get plenty of meat for the three households. Incidentally, hunting buddy number one) shot a twenty-gauge Remington automatic shotgun, and hunting buddy number two shot a 243 Remington bolt action rifle. I got lucky over these fifty-two years that I have hunted in Arkansas with bagging 369 deer in Arkansas but also having killed four really outstanding bucks over these years. And would you believe, these big bucks were all killed within a fifteen-mile radius of Arkadelphia. (Pictures will follow at the end.)

As I told you earlier, my buddies and I never had cameras attached to trees to see what and how many deer might be seen in an area. In fact, tree cameras were not even suggested as a new way of seeing deer without being there until the last fifteen or twenty years in this area. We never put out corn, mineral blocks, or anything to entice the deer to one place to be shot while they were eating. I might add, this can become a pretty involved and expensive method with cameras costing about $100 more or less and, in 2020, a 25# sack of corn sold for about $7.50 a bag. I should also add that other animals like wild hogs, coons, and squirrels, will also eat the corn and consume it in a hurry. I know most have thought my buddies and I have been pretty ignorant to not use these modern devices, but, somehow, I always thought it would be like "taking candy from a baby" or "dirty pool" to draw a deer to corn and shoot it. I just could never see the sport in that kind of hunting for myself. I always figured the deer should be met on their own grounds and that to pit your own mind, hard work, thoughts, shooting ability, etc., was a more sporting endeavor. The truth is that a poor schoolteacher and the two buddies without much education would find it difficult to have the money required to do that kind of hunting. Yes, we did have to spend many more hours in the woods, but seeing all the "wonderful creatures of God in nature" has been worth the long, early, cold, harsh days we spent in the beautiful woods. We never had a box stand either, with or without a heater and all the other comforts of life. We just felt blessed to have these little seven- and eight-foot wooden stands, which I described earlier, and later some sixteen-foot open-air metal stands. We also had one another as good buddies who would go the second or undemanded mile to help.

CHAPTER 11

Deer Hunting Seasons and Weapons

Bows

As I have mentioned, there are three types of deer seasons in Arkansas. Around very late September or by October 1, the bow season opens, and, as I discussed earlier, there are many types of bows; however, the two types most frequently used are the compound bow, which is strictly a manual pull bow, and the crossbow, which has now become such a strong pull that there are usually automatic cockers on most modern high-speed hunting bows. The compound bow requires the hunter to pull different pounds and hold until ready to release the arrow; in other words, more physical strength is required at the instant a potential deer is expected to be close enough to shoot. A crossbow, on the other hand, started out as an old folks' bow because you could pull the string or cable back, lock it into place, and wait for the perfect shot. When deer first came on the scene, a person had to be about sixty-five years old before it was legal to shoot one. After the string or cable was locked into a cocked position, it made it almost identical to shooting a gun because when you pulled the trigger, the arrow was launched at the deer. These became such fascinating, powerful, and deadly weapons, with all the manufacturing companies using methods to build them stronger and faster with cables instead of strings. Many hunters desired to have one, and they became legal for all hunters with a license to hunt. At the present time, any hunter qualified to buy and use a gun can buy and use these crossbows that send an arrow out at an unbelievable speed, and the blades on the ends of the arrows are as deadly as a bullet. Just as with a gun, if an arrow hits vital organs, the deer will bleed internally and die almost always as rapidly as if it were a high-powered bullet from a big caliber gun.

It is not clear where and when the crossbow originated, but it has retained the same basic design as in medieval times. Theirs were for warfare, whereas today, they are basically used for hunting game.

Bow hunting has become very popular, and it can be used through bow, muzzleloader, or modern gun season. It is always legal until the end of deer season when all deer seasons are closed in Arkansas.

I am not sure how many deer I have killed with a bow. I did have a compound bow for a while until the newer crossbows came on the scene. I bought one of the first to come out, and I am still using it. It is still a manual 175 pound pull, with no automation, like an automatic crank, but I killed a small buck with it this season, and it is still fast enough and powerful enough to kill deer at fairly close ranges. Most hunters would really think it was a dud in 2019, but it is still a great little hunting bow. Since I have gotten so old, it is becoming more difficult to manually pull, and last year, when I had a shoulder replacement, my (hunting buddy number three) devised a very simple method for me to cock the bow with the use of a winch (smile). It worked like a charm!

The experience I had with a little doe that came right under my deer stand is the thing that made me know I must get a crossbow. I watched this little deer for about one hundred yards, and as she came nearer and nearer my eight-foot wooden deer stand, I started drawing the compound bow and holding and holding the string back manually for what seemed eons of time because she did not arrive as quickly as I thought she would, and when she got almost right under my stand, I could not shoot because I had to release the string before she got close enough to shoot since my muscles had gotten too weary to hold the string in the cocked position any longer. She walked right under my stand and bolted away at a very fast pace with a "grin on her face."

If you hit a deer in the lungs with an arrow, it will fall dead on the spot; however, it has been my experience, if you hit other vital organs, it may run about forty yards before falling, but you will have visible signs of a death blow if he lowers his tail, the thump sound of an arrow, stumbling, or other signs you will usually observe with a hit deer. Early one morning before I had to go to my job, I dropped my first "dead on the spot" bow deer with a lung shot. That amazed me, and it made my loading and getting to work very early because there was no searching a blood trail forty yards.

I have always tried to keep an accurate record of the number of deer I have killed with the bow, and that was an easy task, to a point, because if I killed one also with the muzzleloader and modern gun in the same year, the Game and Fish Commission would send me a coveted Triple Trophy Award because not many hunters hunt with all three methods through all three seasons. I only hunted one time with a young man who preferred to hunt with a bow all seasons. This may be my last year to hunt because of the aging process, but I did get the seventeenth Triple Trophy Award this year for killing a deer with all three methods. The number may not be completely accurate, but it would be very close.

Muzzleloaders

To me, the muzzleloader is a wonderful weapon, although it is the most sensitive and may let you down because of a misfire if you are not very careful in the handling of your gun. I don't think I have ever had over five misfires in all the years I have used these guns. You are aware, I am sure, that muzzleloaders have been around for a long, long time. They originated in 1364 and were primarily weapons for man until the introduction of handguns in the 1800s. As with all weapons, the early ones were pretty crude, and today, the modern ones are as accurate and deadly as any modern weapon. I now will talk beneath the reader who knows all about muzzleloaders. To get to the point, muzzleloaders are loaded from the muzzle of the gun, and the proper procedure is to put an accurate amount of premeasured black powder down the barrel (muzzle). Hunters, at first, had to use devices such as powder horns to carry the loose black powder, and later the powder was compressed into pellets for easier handling and carrying. They were put down the barrel, and then the bullet was forced (flat end first), down the barrel, with a ram rod, to rest on the powder. Then one must go to the butt end of the barrel and push, into the fire hole, a firing cap, so when the gun is cocked and the trigger pulled, the firing pin hits the firing cap and the spark causes an explosion inside the gun, to launch and propel the bullet to its target. These muzzleloaders have become better and better, and the improvements have made them very popular.

I will digress a moment to say the four "wall hangers" (really big deer) I have killed and had mounted have all been killed with a muzzleloader, and I don't really know why because I have always hunted with all methods as much as I could every season. I think, perhaps, it is due to the time of the seasons since it is our first real gun season of the year, and it is preceded only by bow season. The pressure from much hunting has not yet arrived since fewer people bow hunt. Usually, the last of the modern gun season, we have another quiet time in the woods because most hunters have a job and they have used most of their hunting vacation time and have either not scored, killed all the deer they want, or have become disinterested. I have always hunted every day of every season, except on Sundays, that I could find even a short stretch of time to hunt. Many days, when I was teaching and chairing the biology department, I would arise really early and go to the woods nearby and hunt a couple of hours before I had to be on duty.

You can see how impressed I have been with the three different muzzleloaders I have had, but I did mention very early in this discussion that they will sometimes misfire which means that when you pull the trigger, the gun makes a popping, or fairly loud, sound, much less than the big boom you have with black smoke everywhere when it fires as it should. You have heard the old expression (probably a woman thing), "keep your powder dry." Well, how about this scenario: You may bring your gun in your house where it is cozy and warm at the end of a day's hunt and decide you will load it the next morning when you get up or the night before so you can get an early start in the morning. You jump out the door into twenty-degree weather, put your gun in the cold truck, crank up, and get the heater going full speed ahead, and you may have now put the gun through enough warm and cold conditions that just enough moisture (sweat) has formed that the powder is damp and will not fire completely. Yes, I have had five misfires in my life, and this is only one example of what can cause a misfire; however, if the powder is not kept dry, this is a condition that will cause your mouth to fly wide open (with a few choice words) as that big buck smiles and flies away! Oh, my, what a terrible feeling, but if you muzzleload long enough, you will surely have a misfire with a muzzleloader sooner or later, and you may not even know why.

Although Muzzleloaders are much like a bow because you have only one quick shot, I do love muzzleloader hunting and looking at that dead deer when the black smoke settles, and I see that monster buck lying still on the ground (smile).

Shotguns and Rifles

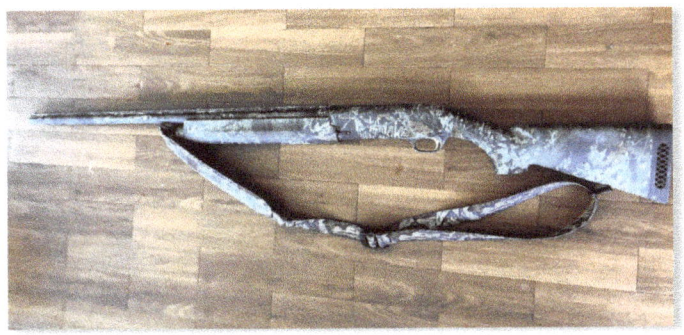

I have told you enough about my early life and how all the Dorris boys had a shotgun when I grew up and first learned to hunt, so you will remember, as a kid, I knew how hard that twelve-gauge automatic shotgun was going to kick me when I pulled the trigger, but I also knew I had to suffer the consequences in order to "run with the big boys" and kill deer. They were big caliber shotguns, and they could shoot one big lead ball (slug) or shells full of smaller lead balls. Slugs shot more like a rifle, but different hunters liked different things, depending on whether they were hunting big game or small game. It was always whether they were hunting in thickets or open zones of timber, etc. The slug was a little better choice for hunting deer in more open spaces, much like a projectile shot from a rifle. You also had to be a little more accurate. Since I grew up in the

Mississippi Delta where there were massive stands of hardwood trees, most of our hunters shot slugs or 00 shells that had several big round lead balls inside instead of shells used for small game. Deer were usually shot at closer ranges than with slugs or rifle bullets. Today, many have chosen modern powerful rifles for deer hunting with only one big lead bullet instead of using shotguns. The big advantage of a shotgun is that it can be used for quail, squirrels, doves, ducks, geese, and other smaller animals, in addition to deer.

These guns have been around a long time and have always proved to be a gun made for woman, man, or child because there are so many types, sizes, and gauges ranging from single shots to automatic firing, and they have and will always be around. More deer hunters have probably used a shotgun more than any other gun over the years; however, high-powered rifles might be the preference at this time.

Young children wishing to hunt are usually started with .22 rifles or 410-gauge shotguns, because they are smaller, lighter weight, safer, and don't have much, if any recoil (kick back). If they turn out to be avid deer hunters, they will quickly advance to higher gauge shotguns, like the twelve-gauge or to larger more powerful rifles such as a 30-06, 308, or 7mm08. There are so many gauges, sizes, and options out there now that hunters have a very wide variety of modestly priced to very high-priced weapons and guns for pleasure. I have only listed a few types of ammunition which I have used over the years, but the list is endless. The types are also endless: shell sizes are also endless. Some people prefer single shot rifles or shotguns, some prefer automatics, some prefer double-barrel shotguns, but most have single barrel, some like rifles that are bolt action, some like automatics, some like lever actions, and on and on. One thing for sure is that you can find just about any kind of shotgun or rifle your heart desires at any gun store, gun catalogue, etc. The sources are endless, as is true with ammunition types, brands, and sizes, etc.

Pistols

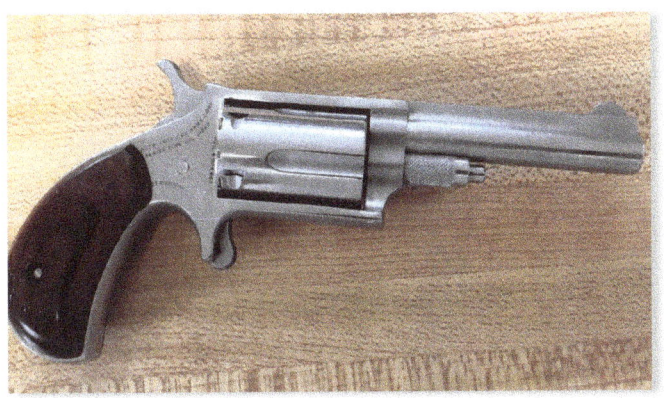

Yes, I did actually buy myself a beautiful .44 Magnum Smith and Wesson nickel-plated revolver pistol with a red dot scope and a six-inch barrel. "It was truly a thing of beauty, but not a joy forever" for me. My first thought was that after I had killed all the deer I wanted with the other artillery, I would like to hunt with a pistol with a telescopic red dot scope. It would be good sport, I thought. I hunted with it a few times, but it was so heavy and so loud that I quit that kind of hunting pretty soon. It truly was a beautiful and worthy pistol and shot a bullet big enough to kill almost anything. Of course, another disadvantage was that you could not shoot the distance with a pistol that you could with a longer barreled muzzleloader, rifle, or shotgun. I decided I would give it to my youngest and strongest hunting buddy (number three) because he had grown from the little fellow who shot rabbits for his mother and himself from the time he was put on the street at twelve years old, and he had always been my young hunting buddy who had developed into a master hunter, and we have had so many good times hunting and fishing together. He still keeps in contact, though he doesn't live here, and we still get together for a few hunts every year, and he continues to call and check on me almost daily. He is truly a deserving person, friend, and hunter, and I know he will cherish it even if he, like I, decides it is not the hunting weapon he would prefer.

I have two other pistols. I mentioned my very small American Arms .22 Magnum pistol which has a 2 1/4 inch barrel. It is my little pocket pistol that I carry almost everywhere, but I especially love having it in my pocket when I go hunting, for all the reasons I mentioned under the category of things a hunter should have in his pocket, bag, or fanny pack and the reasons why.

The other pistol I have is a .38 special Smith and Wesson revolver. You could call it my bedside pistol. I guess I still remember us living so far in the country, and my dad always had a pistol under his mattress for "boogers in the night" and so my mother, who was never a hunter, could protect my brother and me when we were too young to hunt. I will have to tell you one more thing about my mother. Although she didn't hunt, she was a real trooper and put up with many bad things like helping dress the game and fish, and she could cook that venison and everything else in a way that no one else could. She was a grand person to put up with three hunters in her own house and all Dad's brothers who just found it convenient to come by day or night to chat, eat, or swap "big" deer stories, etc. She loved us! Usually, it is mothers who make it possible for their families to have full and enjoyable lives while they stay home and keep the home fires burning. Never ever forget those who are responsible for episodes such as these found in this book because it is true that "the hand that rocks the cradle is the one that rules the world."

Impact of Other Animals on Deer and Man

Bears and Deer

My hunting buddies and I all had deer stands which we referred to by name. The one I will refer to in this topic will be the *bear stand*. It was behind the oldest Baptist Church in the Red River Association in Arkansas. Sometimes, we referred to it as the *church stand*.

Years ago, before my time, there were many black bear in Arkansas, but over the years, they became extinct in this area, and several years ago, the Fish and Wildlife Service intentionally restocked large numbers in many areas of our state. I suppose they can be found in most counties, if not all.

On one of my deer hunts, I saw a young mother bear and her cub late one afternoon from the stand mentioned above. There was a narrow body of water called Pole Cat Branch which ran right behind my stand. They were just walking to this branch from a white oak wooded area. When they arrived on the branch, right behind my stand, I had never heard such blowing, stomping, running, and wheezing by a multitude of deer just ready to cross the branch into that white oak timber. I was too late getting my cell phone out of my pocket to get a picture. Needless to say, they scared all the deer. It was a massive number of deer just ready to cross the branch, almost at the foot of my stand. I think they were as astounded as I. Bear have really made a comeback in Arkansas after many years of devoid populations. Needless to say, "I never got a gunshot for the deer nor a camera shot for the bear, but the love of just seeing such wonderful creatures was worth sitting quietly in a very cold temperature to behold the wonders of nature given for our enjoyment."

Cougars (Panthers, Mountain Lions) and Deer

Many changes in animal populations have taken place during my hunting years in Arkansas. For all the many years I have been in Arkansas, the Arkansas Fish and Game Commission would not admit we had cougars (mountain lions or panthers) in Arkansas. Finally, only this year did they actually admit they were here. It doesn't matter which name you call them, I have been seeing them off and on all the years I have been here. Once I made a plaster of Paris cast in a foot track, and twice I had two very visual encounters. Once I was coming home from an alligator pond that a former superintendent of schools owned. He had invited my herpetology class (study of reptiles and amphibians) to his pond so we could view the alligators that he "called up" by whooping loudly and throwing marshmallows on the water. It was amazing! I decided on a later date to take my hunting buddies (number one and two) to see the alligators in the pond, and as we were leaving by way of a narrow wooded road, a cougar went across the road right in front of us at dusky dark. The long tail was flashing as the cougar crossed the dirt road, entering the wooded area right in front of us, so I did have two eye witnesses. Having taught field zoology and having studied all vertebrates, I knew what I had seen, and I knew cougars were here many years long before the Fish and Wildlife Service finally agreed. In addition, I knew another very reliable hunter who just recently told me he had seen one while hunting. I have seen many bobcats on hunting trips, but I have never seen a cougar while hunting. Another incident that I saw, with my own eyes, occurred as I was baling hay in a rather small pasture, with a creek running through. It was getting pretty late in the afternoon, and I saw a small yearling deer run across the hay field to drink from the creek. Immediately, a cougar was right on top of the deer. It picked that little deer up and kept slamming it against the bank of the creek until it had conquered and killed it for a feast. Such a sad sight, but as a biologist, I realized it was a part of the web of life and the food chain.

Speaking of different kinds of cats, one of the prettiest smaller cats, called bobcats, did one of the most unbelievable things I have ever witnessed. I am sure the wind blowing a little had prevented him from smelling me. I was sitting on the upper 2 x 4 railing of an old rotted wooden box stand about eight feet tall, that a young man had built years before, when he was allowed to hunt on this land behind the church (close to our *bear stand*). I had leaned a ladder from one of our old wooden stands against the tree and the remains of the old rotted box stand. As I sat on one of the 2 x 4s that held the old box stand together, a beautiful bobcat ran under the old box that no longer had a bottom, and he stood there without ever seeing or smelling me. I thought, *My, what an experience.* I would never in a life time have believed he would have lingered without smelling me. When he left, he just cautiously walked away. Animals have to be very wary when the wind blows because they can't detect what direction the odor is coming from, and they must know this to survive. It was a relief to get back to our sixteen-foot metal stands because the old eight-foot wooden stands required us to turn, twist, and contort our bodies to get on the seat from the last step up. The metal stands have a wide top step before the seat so you can just turn around and sit down. The old torn up wooden box stand with only a 2 x 4 to sit on left me with pain in the rear. Just remember, when you love deer hunting, you will sit on anything (smile).

I felt I had to tell you about the above cat because not all cats are dangerous to people nor deer, and my motto is, "Stay in the woods and you will behold more beauty, wonder, and exquisiteness of creation than you can imagine, in addition to the serene beauty of life, from the lowest to the highest forms." Most animals are only trying to live with and not to kill man. Man is actually man's worst enemy. Lower forms are just trying to survive in habitats that man has invaded.

Coyotes and Deer

I would like to make you aware of one thing to think about by relating experiences I have had with coyotes. They, too, can be a real hindrance as predators of deer and other animals.

One late afternoon, my little hunting buddy (number one), with the withered arm and small hand, and I went hunting at the Patterson place, which joined the four hundred-acre Welch mixed tree-covered land, and, just before dark, I shot a big doe and a big yearling at the same place and time because my little buddy was begging me to get more meat for the next year for the family and to help fill the three tags we had left among the three of us; otherwise, I would not have shot a doe that had a yearling with her. Well, it was almost dark, and I had no four-wheeler at that time, so I said I can carry that yearling on my shoulders to my truck (it was not really a long way, and I was young and strong in those early days). I said, "It is very cold tonight, and the big doe will keep until tomorrow morning." We can go at daylight in the morning and get Buddy (number two) to help with the big doe. Would you believe that our mouths flew wide open when we discovered early that next morning that the coyotes had been there during the night, and there was nothing left but a pile of bones and some skin and hair? The coyotes had cleaned those bones and had a meal for themselves. Coyotes are real predators of other game animals and will sometimes steal and eat calves from cattle farms. I should have told you earlier that they usually hunt in packs, and when I had cows, I did have one incident of one very young coyote in the pasture with a group of my sleeping cows late in the afternoon. I immediately ran it away and never had any deaths by cows from coyotes. The man that got me into the cattle business said he had seen one eating out of his cow troughs. Since that incident, I have witnessed a coyote chasing a deer through the woods. It is a known fact that they hunt in packs and kill deer and other animals.

One other coyote incident was an experience my brother had on a muzzleloader hunt. He came down from his deer stand right at dark and had a large group of coyotes looking him over really well, but they didn't attack. That's when he decided to always carry a pistol, as I had suggested, when bow and muzzleloader hunting because you only have one shot. Since his incident, I have read several articles, and I am not sure there is a record of them attacking a human, but the literature said if they are very hungry, it might be a possibility.

This above incident was a real education for me, but the truth is that I had never before left a deer in the woods overnight either. I tried to console myself and my buddies by saying, "Well, coyotes have to eat too, and at least the meat didn't go to waste. We have just experienced again the way the food chain works."

Wild Hogs and Deer

Over the last ten years or so, in this region, wild hogs have just about taken over some of our best hunting lands, especially in low-lying areas where rivers and other streams abound. They destroy deer habitat and take over territories by making mud holes, by rooting up the ground, and by other noxious activities. Many big crops near low-lying areas are completely destroyed. Some would say that the use of corn by deer hunters, with automated feeders, as I have described elsewhere, may be a factor in drawing in the hogs who will eat almost any food source and who reproduce in large numbers. Basically, they eat the corn intended for the deer!

It is ironic that my young buddy (number three) has become so obsessed by the detrimental action and rapid reproduction of hogs in his hunting areas that he has put out some corn and has also put out a large trap to capture them because he believes they are eating all the corn intended for the deer. He kills them and gives the meat to some who are hungry and need meat, after he has shot all he wants for his own freezer. Being the avid hog hunter that he is, he has killed many hogs weighing over 300 pounds. Even the Arkansas Game and Fish Commission has realized the need for some kind of control. These wild hogs destroy not only crops but also animal and plant populations and habitats in some of our better hunting areas. They usurp both food and space which deer populations have formerly used. At this writing, and in this area, there is no season on hogs; they may be killed any time, by anyone with or without a hunting license.

CHAPTER 13

Hunting Clubs

Hunting Club #1

Several years after I moved to Arkadelphia, I decided I would join a hunting club in Joan, Arkansas, which was about eight miles from Arkadelphia. I decided it would broaden my horizon and hunting opportunities in other land areas. My hunting buddies (number one and two) did not have the money to join a hunting club, so I joined without them. There were approximately twenty members, but no camp house nor any type building, so the dues strictly went for some land area we could hunt. I killed some good deer there, and the people were great, but I did miss my hunting buddies. We never had dogs to run the deer or anything like that; we just put up deer stands on trees and hunted. I will digress to tell you, however, that in all my hunting years in and out of Arkadelphia, we never used dogs to run the deer, but in the Mississippi Delta, everyone ran dogs, and some clubs in and around Arkadelphia run them too. There is an advantage in hunting with dogs because they jump the deer out of their beds, and when you hear them barking and running, you know there is a deer in front of them, but you know me, just give me a quiet peaceful place, and I can stay in the woods all day, just watching and waiting to observe anything of interest to a biologist. I never had deer dogs nor the time to train them, so I learned to go into the woods and sit in those places I had scouted and knew deer were using for food, water, bedding, safe areas, etc. I also feel that dogs put much fear into deer, and man has an unsporting advantage.

Back to the hunting club, I never killed a really big "wall hanger" there, and I did continue to hunt with my buddies back in our regular places in Arkadelphia, and I did kill a really big twelve-point buck while I was in that hunting club, but it was in Arkadelphia and not on the hunting club land. Anyway, this young guy in the club was just beginning to take a taxidermy course, and he stayed on my heels to "Please let him mount that twelve-point buck." He just kept begging and bugging me to let him mount the deer.

I didn't have much money on hand then, but my mother and father had come from Mississippi for a visit in 1990. I had just cut off the big twelve-point rack, and when my dad heard the story, though a man who had hunted all his life and had big racks hanging on all our walls where I grew up, he blurted out, "Yes, you will have that head mounted, and I will pay for it myself." He went on to say, "Many people hunt a lifetime and never kill a deer that good."

So, reluctantly, I carried the deer rack to this young guy who had never mounted a head before, and he did a pretty sorry job, but considering the fact that he had no experience, I guess it was not just terrible, especially for the price of $75. Today the going rate, in this area, is $400 or more for each of the other two professional mounts shown in this paper and hanging on my wall. Well, at least, he got some experience, and I stayed in this club for two years, and then I heard of another club in the same area which I decided to join.

Hunting Club #2

The second club which I joined was just a few miles down the road from club number one, and I thought the timber included a little more hardwood and good browse for the deer. I decided to check it out, so I took my buddies (number one and number two) along to survey the situation, knowing all the time that they did not have money to join a club and they would have to stay with our original program hunting on bits and pieces of private property owned by people they knew in Arkadelphia who had the goodness in their hearts to let us hunt all those years. One of them now had a used four-wheeler, so they faithfully helped me look the lease situation over, with the club owner having us follow behind him, on our four-wheelers, as he rode his four-wheeler and showed us around the lease. He pointed out some good places to hunt and to put a stand. He also had a nice little club building with a pot-bellied wood stove and a few chairs so the hunters could have a place to gang around and warm themselves after a cold hunt. They could also tell big tails like how many deer they saw, the big one that got away, and all sorts of things that hunters talk about. If someone killed a deer, there was a good place to hang the deer to dress it and brag a little. The camp actually was not set up for sleeping with beds, bunks, etc., but most members lived close around anyway. It would have been possible to bring along a bed roll, sleeping bag, or something to bunk there if one wished; however, I never knew anyone who did because I think all the members were local and found their beds at home a more comfortable place than that concrete slab to sleep on and the iron pot-bellied stove to have to keep stoking with wood to have heat all night. Occasionally, I would take one or both of my hunting buddies for a hunt at the club, but nonpaying members were not encouraged.

Despite this fact, this turned out to be a surprising situation for me. I found another wonderful hunting buddy (number three), much younger than I but very anxious to learn how to deer hunt; however, I certainly did not desert my original hunting buddies (number one and number two). It was nice to have a twenty-one-year-old learner when I was sixty-one years old. It was also wonderful to see him grow in his hunting ability, and he eventually became one of the best people and hunters with whom I have ever hunted. Over the next many years, he has repaid my feeble efforts toward him and given me back more help, happiness, and good memories than I could ever express.

C H A P T E R   1 4

Hunting Buddy (Number 3)

It was my first day to hunt the new lease, and everyone met at the camp very early in the morning having already put their stands in the suggested places by the camp owner. I will digress again to tell you that my new twenty-one-year-old hunting buddy (number three) was being shown the lease by the owner the same day my other buddies and I were shown around and given locations for good stands.

Now, on our first day at the new lease, we all left the camp going to our stands down this four-wheeler trail. I had the first stand on the little dirt road, and other young new members of the club had their deer stands farther down the road. Most of the newer members were on this road, but there were other dirt roads through that eighty-acre plot on which the other members had put their stands years ago. Most had been members for several years (and I figured might have the best spots). Most of the new members were probably eighteen to twenty-one years old. Fairly early, there were only a few shots heard, but these young new members were getting cold and tired and had not fired a shot. They all decided they would go back to that camp about ten thirty because it was bitter cold, and I knew that pot-bellied camp stove looked mighty good and promising in their thoughts. They were probably also hungry and very inexperienced. Since my stand was the first on that four-wheeler trail, it was obvious they would come by me before getting to the camp house. As each one on his four-wheeler came clattering by me (there were about four or five), I had some pretty bad thoughts, but I was not one to use bad language. All I could think of was that these inexperienced young men on their four-wheelers were a real noisy nuisance, and the noise would scare any deer away that had any thoughts of coming by my stand. Well, I sat there, with bad thoughts, knowing that any seasoned hunter would never think of leaving a stand before eleven or twelve o'clock. About eleven fifteen, surely enough, here came a nice seven-point buck. I shot him and loaded him on my four-wheeler, which I had parked close to my stand in the woods. I covered it with my camouflaged cover, which was a very good blend right in the woods not too far behind my deer stand. As I came to the camp house, there were several men still standing around, warming themselves, talking, laughing, telling tall tales, etc. I just said, as I stopped for a moment, "Well, boys, you left your stands too early," smiled, and rode my four-wheeler up on my folding ramp into the back of my pickup truck with the deer on the back rack of the four-wheeler. I went home, called my other two hunting buddies (number one and number two), and had them meet me at my cow pasture so we could use our great "Bloodless Golf Ball" method of dressing a deer (see chapter 9).

An Early Hunt at the Second Hunting Club

This second hunting lease was the last one I ever joined. My new twenty-one-year-old buddy (number three), very early in the season, shot his first deer and must have hit him only in the front leg. I was going to help him hunt it and show him how to blood trail a deer to see if I could help him find the deer. Before I go on with this tale, I would like to say, "If you are new to deer hunting, and if you have never wounded or killed a deer, I feel you must, above all things, be an ethical deer hunter, and if you think you might have wounded or killed a deer, you must pursue the locating of it as soon as possible to put it out of its misery." And now, back to the story of my young hunting buddy who said, "I think I blew its leg off." Well, I knew that if he had just made a leg shot, the deer would not be found, and it, for sure, would not be dead. I went with him to his stand, and we did find a few drops of blood, so I showed him how, if the deer was not bleeding profusely, he might have to get down on his hands and knees and look very hard at every leaf, every bare spot on the ground, every nearby bush, tree, etc., to see if he could keep following the blood. We did not find his deer, as I suspected. Being older and more experienced, this gave me a real chance to say, "Don't you ever shoot a deer unless you are pretty sure you have a 'death shot' or a 'vital shot' which, hopefully, will kill the deer almost instantly, without pain and suffering." My prayer each time I hunt is: "Help it to be a quick clean kill, without pain and suffering." I think that is such an important thing to keep in mind when hunting any animal. To leave an animal to suffer and die, or, even worse, to leave a wounded deer to be attacked by a predator and killed after being wounded is such a terrible thought and such a dastardly thing to happen when hunters only wound a deer. That is why I believe so much that one should not shoot unless they know it can be a lethal shot and not a wounding shot. Anyway, I will end this topic by saying, no, we didn't find his deer, but he did learn a lesson about tracking deer and about doing the right thing before pulling that trigger.

The Life and Experiences of a Great Deer Hunter (3)

I want to tell you what a blessing it has been to always have a good hunting buddy. My young twenty-one-year-old hunting buddy was truly a blessing in disguise, because when the first two hunting buddies got older, weaker, and disabled in certain ways, they had to stop hunting, and I would have been hunting completely alone my last ten years, if it had not been for my young buddy coming along. He was a very quick and astute learner when it came to hunting and all the things that go with being a desirable hunter. He was rather alone in the world because his father or the man he lived with threw him and his mother out on the streets when he was about twelve years old. He had an old .22 rifle and shot rabbits, squirrels, and anything else he could find for them to eat. So he really came up with a gun in his hands, and he was ready to have a coach who was older to hunt with him, and I was surely anxious to have him go with me. I can tell you right now that for one of my stature, about five feet four inches tall (as I am now), it is somewhat a chore to do all the things necessary to make things convenient for hunting, like putting up and moving sixteen-foot metal deer stands, dragging them around to change locations, cutting out shooting lanes, and removing logs, trees, and other noxious things that the harsh months of winter bring before the hunt begins the next year. One of the really hard chores for me has occurred, in my older age, when I killed a real wall hanger like the one I killed this year or a deer so large that it almost took two people to load it. My young hunting buddy was always there. He is now forty-six, and I am eighty-six, and you had better believe that his youth and strength have made my hunting go on and on without all the woes of most older people.

Now, I am going to surprise you with what I will be writing next. Earlier in this book, I described to you many types of weapons, tree stands, and other desirable ways of hunting deer. Well, I want to say, on the front end of what I am about to describe, that this young buddy has learned to use some very modern and different modes of hunting than those I have used all my life and have described to you throughout this book.

I alluded earlier to the fact that the corn feeding method is desirous to many young people who are still in the workforce and probably don't have as much time to spend in the woods as I. Having a big box stand high up in the air is also convenient and comfortable because you can have a comfortable swivel chair, heater, thermos of coffee, food, water, and anything you might desire to keep dry and warm in our twenty- to forty-degree temperatures during the winter months. Some hunters keep corn out by various methods. If they cannot afford to buy big bulky metal stands with an automated corn feeding container on top that will hold a couple of bags of corn or more, and will be activated by battery to start a fan which will throw corn at certain intervals of time (these automatic feeders do come in different sizes), then they may just scatter corn on the ground or put piles of it near their stands. Many hunters, who use the corn method and/or keep out mineral blocks for the deer, would never want to go back to my old rustic method of outdoor hunting unless they didn't have the money for this newer method or the challenge of the older method. Now, if you have the money, you can also buy tree cameras which attach to trees and cost about $100, more or less. And guess what, if you look at the pictures they make, you can tell what deer (bucks, does, yearlings, etc.) have passed by your stand and if they tarried to eat your corn. So I want you to be aware of newer and easier methods of hunting white tail deer because, although it may cost you dearly, you will usually have to hunt less time and under much more desirable conditions to kill a deer. Again, I have expressed my opinion and told you earlier that I never gave up the old rustic method of "mixing it with the deer" in their own environment, because I just felt it gave them more of a chance and took a little more effort which ultimately brought me more pride. I do, however, want you to be apprised of newer methods too.

My buddy (number three) has moved on in his life and now lives about forty-five miles from Arkadelphia, so we don't get to hunt together nearly as much as when he lived here in Arkadelphia. He not only can afford to use the more modern methods of hunting, as described in the above paragraph, but he has killed more deer than most could imagine. He is married, and in his home, you will see many good deer heads hanging on his walls. My collection of "wall hangers" will also be on his walls when I die. He is a great hunter, with a wonderful 308 Browning rifle and a 7mm08 rifle. His wife is also a wonderful hunter who has killed many deer. In addition to the above, he also manages a fairly large deer camp near Hot Springs, Arkansas, where he lives and hunts. He knows all the right things and how to manage such endeavors. Although he has many deer in the vicinity of his camp, and can run to a stand many days after work and on weekends, he still finds time to come to Arkadelphia on some weekends and holidays to hunt with me, his old hunting buddy. In fact, on the next to the last day of the hunting season this year, he and I hunted on the eighty-acre Arkadelphia plot, which he rents, and it is the same acreage we hunted on when we both joined the second hunting club, and he was twenty-one and I was sixty-one in the year 2001. There are still many old wooden deer stands too rotted and broken to use since that land was rented at least once or twice after we left the lease. I believe it will always be a wonderful place to hunt.

This past modern gun season on November 20, 2018, I killed my last big "wall hanger buck" at fifteen minutes before dark on this very plot of land that my young buddy has rented so we can have an occasional hunt here when he has time to come to Arkadelphia to hunt. Without his help, I would have had a very hard time bringing this deer out of the woods. It is a phenomenal thing that this is where we both first started hunting together, where I killed two of the mounted "wall hangers" and where I may have ended my hunting career. He has certainly been a true friend and a great hunter. By the way, he had not put out corn on that plot that we were hunting this year (big smile).

Overcoming Obstacles with Good Friends

Arkansas hunting grounds have many ravines, and I grew up in the Mississippi flat delta land, near the Mississippi River where flooding was so common at times that one could not hunt because of the vast amounts of water. Arkadelphia is a totally different place with many hills, hollows, and deep ravines. I especially remember two of my favorite hunting locations where there were many ravines. One spot in the Shiloh Community which I called my *honey hole* (because I killed so many deer there), but right across the highway, I had another which I called the *baby stand* or *ravine stand* because I had seen so many babies and mothers there and there were so many ravines.

In addition to all the ravines, there are many other obstacles which I had to overcome when my hunting buddies were no longer able to accompany me through my deep desire to deer hunt for as long as I could pull the trigger. These ravines always posed problems for one person to retrieve dead deer.

Friend A

The first obstacle relates to a kill in which the doe I had shot with my 30-06 rifle fell into a deep small ravine. I could not get her out, so

I called a university friend since my main hunting buddies, number one and number two, were no longer able to hunt, and my buddy number three had moved. We did get the deer out, but we had to go into the ravine, cut the deer into quarters, and lift each piece out, piece by piece (with one down in the ravine and one on the bank above). The ravine was so deep I could not pull the deer out with the winch on my four-wheeler. This is also the friend who insisted on paying for having my last "wall hanger" buck mounted. Good friends are priceless!

Friend B

After I lost my first two hunting buddies (number one and number two), and then my young hunting buddy (number three) moved away from Arkadelphia, fortunately, one of my former students had accumulated much land in Clark County, around Arkadelphia, was in my church, and knew that I no longer had a good hunting buddy near, so he invited me to hunt on his land. He also had a big camp on the Ouachita River which ran right through Arkadelphia, but I never really stayed at his camp. His camp was also farther from Arkadelphia than some land he had, which was about ten minutes from my house, and this is where I hunted. He did some things that no other person would have thought of doing. Not only did he show me some good areas to hunt on his land near my home, he also let me hunt some of the good stands at his camp on a few occasions when the members had killed all the deer they wanted and had usually moved out of the camp house. They were very nice stable box stands, and one even had an automatic corn feeder throwing corn at timed intervals and also a cow trough with a salt and a mineral block. One thing I learned early since I had never hunted in these fine box stands was that I was so short that if I sat in those office swivel chairs or other chairs, I could not see over the shooting rail and would have to stand and hunker down on the rail to shoot; however, I never killed a deer from a tower box stand and only hunted in one about four times.

Now, I will have to tell you one of the finest things he ever did was let me use his box stand on slides. It sat on the ground and could be pulled or moved around from place to place. I had just had one of three knee joint replacements during that time and knew I would never be able to climb my sixteen-foot open air deer stands until healing occurred, so he offered this little sliding box stand, which sat in a good pine and hardwood forest so I could sit in comfort and hunt, even in the late afternoon since it was so close to my house. Would you believe that hunting on that first, very cold afternoon, I was warmed by my portable My Buddy Propane Heater, and two deer appeared within shooting distance. Again, it was muzzleloader season, and although it was not a monster buck, I took meat home and thought it was grand and that I was in heaven, despite the fact I had a bum leg.

A few years before the above incident, I was hunting at my honey hole, in the Shiloh Community, and I killed a very large eight-point buck for a retired preacher friend in my church. I shot it with my crossbow as it came across the *honey hole* branch, and it ran back across the branch, the same branch mentioned where I killed the big wide 22 1/2-inch spread mentioned and pictured at the end of the paper. Again, I needed help to get that big buck across that branch, and I called this same friend (my former student) who was now in his sixties. He came immediately, and I did not find out until later that he was having an atrial fibrillation attack. How is that for a friend who will go beyond and above the call of duty for a friend??

It is so important for me to point out one more thing about this great friend: This very year, he had completed his deer kill for the year, and I had no muzzleloader pellets or bullets. When I went out for the last weekend of the modern gun season (on Saturday) and killed the big number four wall hanger (pictured below), it was with his own muzzleloader pellets and bullet, which he had let me have so I would not have to buy a box of pellets and bullets at the end of the season! No matter what one can say or do, "there is nothing like having good friends and hunting buddies."

Friends B and C

I also killed another eight-point buck on the *ravine stand* with my muzzleloader late one afternoon. It took friend B and another friend C from his hunting club (also a member of our church) to get that deer out of a very, very deep ravine. Again, my friend B was here for me. This is what we did: One went down into the ravine to hook the cable that was on the front of my four-wheeler, one stayed on the bank and kept the cable free of grass, limbs, and debris, while I sat on the four-wheeler and held my finger on the winch button. Wow! What a problem! Actually, B went into that deep ravine, and he had only had a recent knee replacement surgery. If you only knew how deep this ravine was and what a struggle it was to retrieve this deer, you would understand what *real friends* are and how they can make a terrible situation seem not really so bad after all.

Friend D

This year, the first day of the bow season, I shot a yearling buck with my crossbow, and it ran right in to a ravine to die. I had no buddies to call upon, so I called a young deer hunter friend. Notice I said "called." It was so nice when cell phones came into being.

I had never hunted with this young man, but knew he had a big 7mm08 rifle with a very powerful telescopic sight, and he had seen some very big deer by using the cameras and corn method this year. He knew also that I was hunting by myself and had been for many years and that sometime I had to depend upon help from friends when I killed a large ravine deer that took two people to remove it. I called this friend, and he helped get the deer out of the ravine. Before he left my truck to come home, he said, "Why don't you come over and muzzleload hunt with me for three days before my brother comes from Little Rock to hunt with me?" We planned a time, after one morning hunt when I could go over to his hunting club acreage. He had four nice stands, two were metal lean-to stands, up against a tree, one was a box stand on a tower, and one a box stand on the ground. His deer lease was in a very good pine/hardwood forest area and had many fire lanes where one could see and shoot long distances. He also had the right gun and scope to take a deer at a very long distance. It was a place somewhat like the place above mentioned, where I used the little box stand on a slide (friend B), except his was not on a slide. Since he put out corn and had cameras, he had some dandy pictures of big bucks, and he had shot at one or two this year at very long distances. A person could shoot four hundred yards down those fire lanes with super equipment like his.

To make a long story short, I did desire to have someone to hunt with, and I just needed one more deer, with the muzzleloader to obtain the Triple Trophy Award again this year to make number sixteen, and I knew that, although I had a very worthy 30-06 rifle, my scope was a $50 scope from Walmart (I never had one that cost more because I shot reasonable distances inside wooded areas, knowing the deer would be close enough to put it on the ground with one shot).

So after thinking about the wonderful offer he had made to let me be his guest on his hunting lease, I had to be truthful, without hurting his feelings, and I said, "I really hate to turn down such a good offer, but I would not feel comfortable shooting such long distances down those fire lanes and my scope is not worthy of shooting that distance!" I think we were both disappointed at my decision, but I hunted the next to the last day of the modern gun season with my muzzleloader, because I had already taken a little buck with my bow and a doe with my rifle (remember, you can always hunt with a lesser weapon during the modern gun season). I guess I made the right decision by hunting on my buddy number three's rented eighty acres where we both joined that club many years earlier. He had come for a hunt with his modern gun, and I opted to take my muzzleloader for one last chance to get the Triple Trophy Award. I was so glad that he was hunting about a mile away and came back at black dark (remember I shot at five fifteen) to help get that deer out. Hooray another trophy (see trophy picture)!

Friend E

One more good friend I will mention is the one upon whom I had to call during the 2017 hunting season to help me get the extremely wide rack trophy deer from the *honey hole* branch. He lived near my *honey hole* stand (mentioned earlier and probably of all stands this was my best). His efforts are mentioned in the trophy deer descriptions below, as are those of other buddies and friends. It took both of us to get the wide rack up the bank from the stream of water (see Trophy Bucks).

Finally, I will say, "Never give your buddies and friends out." And hunting is one of the best things one can do to bring peace and pleasure, put meat on the table, and to learn reverence for nature and the one who gave us all the beautiful and supreme animals and plants, along with our wonderful friends and buddies.

The last two events mentioned above were in 2017 and 2018, and by this time, one of my two original buddies (number one) had died in the nursing home at ninety years, in 2015, and the other one (number two) went into the nursing home that same year, sadly impaired and unable to speak, walk, etc., but they had not been able to hunt for at least ten years. As mentioned before, buddy number three had also moved away, and these years have been very sad years for me because hunting alone is not nearly as much fun nor as safe. You cannot imagine how I have missed and needed them. Again, you will understand this last sentence more when you get to the end of this book.

Friend F

I killed a very large deer right at dark and only a half mile out of Arkadelphia (town) while hunting alone. This is what happened:

A young friend whom I had just met a week before when he saw me park my truck and trailer on the street fairly close to his house as I unloaded my 4 wheeler, came out and said, "if you ever need help, I will help you." About 5:00 last night (Dec. 11, 2019), he was in his yard grilling and heard my 30-06 rifle shot. As I was struggling in the dark with my worn out deer loader, made for smaller deer, he appeared, helped me put the loader back together, jumped up on the back of my 4 wheeler and said, "I am just going to do this like I am used to doing." I was amazed at how strong he was and how he grabbed the back legs of that big deer and bodily pulled it up on to my 4 wheeler back rack. Then, he disappeared on foot with his flashlight, back through the wooded area to his home in town as I traveled the little woods road to my truck and trailer and, lo and behold, he had his truck near my truck with lights shining right down that little muddy road so I would be able to safely arrive and load the 4 wheeler on my trailer with the deer snuggly strapped on the back rack.

The strangest thing of all was that I had learned on our first meeting that his mother-in-law had been one of the smartest and finest biology students and graduate assistants I had ever taught and had in my classes. Friends are our God-given angels, and I shall always gratefully remember his kindness to an old 86 year old deer hunter.

CHAPTER 16

Great Changes Over the Years

Over the many years I have hunted in Arkansas and Mississippi, I have seen many changes, and I would never be able to relate all of them; however, I would like to relate some of the most important that have affected my life. The cell phone, four-wheelers, and all-terrain vehicles have become more available and more advanced, guns, bows, and telescopic sights are more accurate, and hunting attire, scent lock suits, deer populations, and deer stands often have a "rest"

mechanism so one can put the gun across it to prevent movement of the barrel and have a more accurate shot. Climbing tree stands were once very popular in this area, and I owned a couple myself because they offered mobility and the ability to climb up a tree any place desired instead of being situated in only one tree in one place. They are, however, a little burdensome to carry on your back from one place to another and can also be more dangerous if they should not be attached very tightly to the tree you have climbed. I have left mine hanging in my boathouse for several years because as I got older and had to have three knee joint replacements over the years, two shoulder replacements, two wrist surgeries, and one thumb surgery, they became more cumbersome for me to carry. So at this point in my life, I am still dedicated to those sixteen-foot metal open air stands firmly attached to the trees, but new box stands are awesome, though I never owned one. I still admit that those climbing tree stands were mighty handy to throw over your shoulder and just climb any tree you decided if deer changed their paths due to food, water, or other situations. It was really nice to have those portable stands. Today, if I really want to go portable, I can use a small tripod stool which is light and can be put against the butt of a tree or hidden away somewhere so I can swivel the seat and shoot in a pretty wide radius. (I hate to tell you, but after hunting above ground level nearly all my life, it is hard for me, but it does make one very mobile and is easy to carry. My hunting buddy number three is really in love with the mobility of these small stands.)

I can never begin to tell you of all the changes in hunting equipment that are there now for all hunters. Just read lots of catalogues and hunting materials and go to sporting goods stores. You can go "cheap," as I always have, or you can have the equipment and newest changes of a rich person.

Two or three years ago, the elk on the Buffalo River and surrounding areas (counties in Arkansas) got a terrible disease called "wasting disease," and now the disease today has been spread to twelve counties in Arkansas and other surrounding states. The Fish and Wildlife Commission is monitoring this situation very carefully, and so far, the counties around Arkadelphia (Clark and Dallas), where

I hunt, have not been plagued by the disease. These deer with the disease lose much weight and should not be eaten; however, healthy deer can be a wonderful food source. Deer chili, deer hamburgers, deer tenderloin, etc., are great sources of protein for humans and are quite delicious. We even have programs where the hunter can pay slaughterhouses and butchers a minimal fee of $5–$10 and have the deer prepared for food pantries or for others who need food, and it is a good source of protein. I have been blessed to see deer populations increase and to have good hunting conditions with longer hunting seasons and bigger bag limits. Another change for the better is the development of more WMAs (wildlife management areas), which are a blessing in Arkansas. They are wonderful places to hunt, especially if you are looking for great variation and diversity. In most cases, hunters have to draw for permits to hunt certain areas. The bear populations are becoming more and more plentiful due to stocking over the last few years, and there are now regular seasons in which bear can be hunted.

At this point, I would like to interject one more thing I have observed during my long years of hunting and fishing: These are good clean sports, and they keep children off the streets and away from drugs, gangs, and some of the terrible places and things that children are subjected to today.

Changes come and go, but there could never be a more loving thing in life today than for a child to be with a godly parent or a good, clean, and conscientious friend hunting or fishing, instead of being on the streets in devious places or where drugs abound and other bad habits have become so rampant.

C H A P T E R   1 7

Triple Trophy Awards

Over all my fifty-three years in Arkansas, I managed to get a total of 17 Triple Trophy Awards of which I was very proud. This means you have taken a deer with a bow, muzzleloader, and modern gun during one hunting season, which last only from the end of September through early February. Perhaps if I had put out piles of corn, I could have enticed more deer and obtained more trophies, but I used the old method of hunting them on their own terms, and I also had a teaching position at the university, and one or two more jobs most of the time, to say nothing of the fact that I was trying to start from four black Angus cows and artificially breed through four generations to get one hundred head of purebred Simmental cows, which I mentioned earlier. I am just blessed and proud of the ones I have gotten (see pictures).

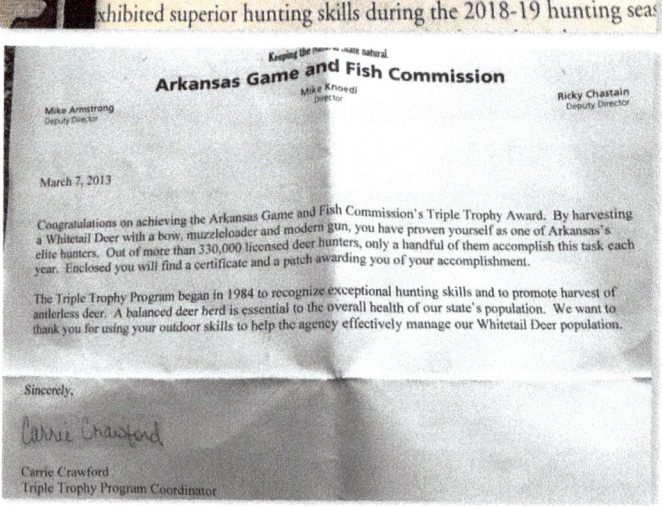

Trophy Bucks over a Lifetime

1990: The Twelve Points—First Wall Hanger and Worst Mount

This big boy had just come from a pond about five in the afternoon, and I was sitting on a log, hunting alone, as was often the case. I saw him just moseying along a fence which surrounded some woods, and very quickly, I pulled the trigger on my .50 caliber Thompson/Center muzzleloader. He fell dead instantly. I always carried a rope and other supplies in a bag on the front rack of my four-wheeler, so I tied a rope to him and dragged him out to the Patterson house where only Mr. Patterson, who was paralytic, and his wife lived. It was dark when I got there, and I knew this was a big twelve-point buck that would be an effort to load into my pickup bed. Mrs. Patterson, being the good woman she was, offered to help, and after straining, puffing, and blowing, we finally got that big boy loaded into my truck (I did not have the deer loader on my first four-wheeler during those early years). I carried him by a deer specialist and asked him how old he thought the deer was. He thought the deer was about seven years old (jaw bones and teeth are used to determine age). I believe most of these big deer that I killed will also be in the range of seven to ten years old. I think the reason I didn't kill more huge deer over the years is that they have been mighty sly to avoid hunters and other predators in order to live this long. This is the one that was mounted by a beginner (alluded to in the body of the paper) who needed a subject to practice on, but he did a fair job for $75, and you can't beat that!

2003: The Fourteen Points—Largest Number of Points Deer Rack

What a monster this deer turned out to be! I, again, was hunting by myself in the second hunting club I joined. About three o'clock, I decided to go to my stand a little early. It was one of those old eight-foot wooden stands we had built and attached to the tree with ratchet straps. I had hunted in it that morning and thought one ratchet strap was a little loose because I could feel a little movement in the seat, so I decided to go early and tighten the ratchet straps on the tree a little before the afternoon hunt. About 5:20, this deer that looked just like a big red Herford cow came walking from the rear and to the right of my stand. I saw him coming about seventy-five yards away, but if he kept his same path, he would pass right to the right of my stand where there was a little grove of small pine trees. I thought to myself, when he comes into the opening right past those little pine trees, I will shoot. I had a perfect shot because he was still just walking and had not smelled nor detected me at all. I pulled the hammer back on my Thompson/Center muzzleloader, fired, and he stumbled and fell about fifty yards from my stand. I heard him crash to the ground just after he crossed a little shallow ditch. Again, it was getting to be almost dark, and I failed to follow the cardinal rule which my dad had always taught me. The rule was to never walk upon a down deer without reloading or having a loaded gun. Well, go back and look at my discussion of the muzzleloader, and you will see a description of how many things you have to do to reload, and it takes a few minutes. I was so sure he was dead, and it was almost dark, and I opted to not reload because I just knew I had a dead deer. As soon as I walked upon him, with his head cuddled into his body, lying still on the ground, he jumped up, bolted, and was away in a flash. I knew he would die as soon as I saw the massive amount of blood on the trail, but I knew I would never find and load him by myself in the dark. The weather was freezing, so I knew the meat would still be good the next day. My young hunting buddy, (number three), and I found him the next morning. Surely enough, he had made a circle and fell dead almost in the spot behind my stand where I had seen him at first. He went home to die. My buddy sawed off his rack, and I waited about four years to have him mounted because I didn't seem to ever have the $400 it took for a professional mount. I took it to a professional in Hot Springs, and I thought he did a wonderful job.

Before I had the rack mounted, I had friends who coaxed me to take it to the Big Buck Classic, held in Little Rock, Arkansas, every year. He would be competing with the best bucks killed that year in Arkansas, and he did get a third place white ribbon and recognition sheet which is framed and on my wall of triple trophies. I was happy with that award because I knew there would be keen competition with many good deer heads presented by many competitors from all over the state. His rack scored 148.4.

2016: Eight Points—Exceptional and Enormous Widespread Rack, 22 1/2 Inches

I was hunting in the Shiloh Community, where my *honey hole* stand was located. I had a stand right there from the beginning of my hunting career in Arkadelphia, and I probably killed more deer there from those first seven- and eight-foot homemade wooden stands than in all the years I have hunted in this area. I had been on that stand since early morning, and, about eleven, I looked straight down a deer trail from my stand, and I saw an extremely wide rack big buck, walking along the little branch of water. My first thought was: *That is the widest rack I have ever encountered in the woods.* I had my ScentLok suit on, as usual, and I would not move a muscle or blink an eye and try to shoot as he looked directly at the stand because I knew he would bolt and run. I stayed very still, and when he made a right turn to continue down the trail, and now at my left side, I shot him with my little inexpensive Wolf muzzleloader since I had literally worn out my two faithful Thompson/Center muzzleloaders and the season was upon us, so I went to the handiest place to buy a muzzleloader in a hurry. It was the only one the store had and a much cheaper gun than I had been using, but it has killed several deer for me, including the one I killed this year, and has turned out to be a good "little meat and potato gun."

I knew I had wounded him mortally, and he took about four more steps and was paralyzed in the branch (wounded deer always go to water, if there is an available stream). He was mortally wounded but not dead. I reloaded my gun, while still on my stand, as fast as I could with my Quick Load. I will digress a moment to say that I always put pellets, firing caps, and bullets in a Quick Load tube so I could reload pretty fast sitting up on the deer stand. I knew he couldn't get up, but I shot a little high, since he was at an angle, and hit him in the spine. I could see him in the deep hole in the water of that narrow branch as he kept moving his antlers up. I told you earlier that I always carried a small pistol for just such things as this. After reloading rapidly, I came down the stand and went to the stream, not more than forty yards from my stand, and shot him with that little pistol. He was not suffering, thank goodness, because he was paralyzed from a spinal shot.

Well, now there was still a problem because he was so large, and his antlers were so wide that I could not winch him out with the winch on the front of my four-wheeler because the banks of the little water branch were so steep that when I would try to winch him or try to pull him with a rope attached to the back of my four-wheeler, the rack would keep catching on the side of the bank. If there had been a tree nearby that I could have thrown a rope over the limb and pulled him up with a rope on the back of my four-wheeler, I could have gotten him out by myself because it would have raised his antlers above the bank of the stream and then I would have used the winch on the front of the four-wheeler to pull him out.

By 2016, my first two hunting buddies (number one and number two) had died or were in the nursing home, and my buddy (number three) had moved away, so I had to get help. I knew another hunter that lived on the other side of that branch, not too far away, and there was a good gravel road to his house. About twelve thirty, I rode my four-wheeler out of the woods to my truck, not parked too far away, took off some of my outer hunting clothes since the temperature was warming up, rode my four-wheeler to his place, and asked if he would help me. He had a larger four-wheeler than mine, and he rode it behind mine until we got to the branch. We then tied my rope to the awesome antlers and his four-wheeler. I then held the rack and head high enough that he could pull the deer out of the branch. He kept saying, "You don't find a buck that big around here and certainly not with a rack that wide." He raised soy beans on his side of the branch and had killed some really good bucks in his fields, so after he kept going on and on about what a wide rack that was, I decided maybe it really was an unusually good kill.

If he, my friend E, hadn't been a mighty strong man, we would not have loaded it on my four-wheeler. We tried to load it naturally on the loader, and it bent the loader, so he almost manually loaded it on the back rack of my four-wheeler by himself. Don't ever forget what I said about good friends!

I was ready now to take the deer fifteen miles to the deer processing place for dressing, cutting, and wrapping. I saw a truck, with two men following me to Bismarck, Arkansas, to the slaughterhouse, processing place, and they came right behind me to that place where I stopped. They jumped out of their truck (they were brothers who had come to pick up a processed cow).

When I stopped to unload my deer, they immediately said, "Will you take a picture of that deer with our cell phones?"

I did and then asked if they would take a picture of me with my cell phone. The boy who unloaded the deer called to his boss and said, "I think you ought to see this!"

Well, by now, I was beginning to believe I must have a pretty big deer with an unusually wide rack. It truly was one of the biggest deer, with the widest rack I had ever killed, and most people recognized that fact before I did.

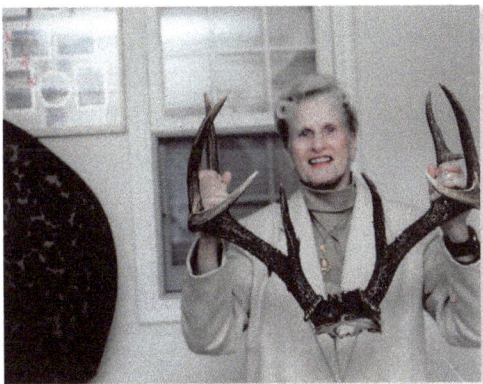

2018: The Eight Points—My Last Monster Buck

This buck will always be one of the greatest memories of my life for several reasons. On Saturday, the next to the last day of the modern gun season this year, my hunting buddy (number three), who has moved to Hot Springs and is involved with his family, job, managing a big deer hunting club, entering and winning many fishing tournaments in a town with three big lakes, running a cattle farm, etc., still invites me to hunt with him because he also has eighty acres rented in Joan where he and I joined hunting club (number two). He called me on Friday night and said he would like us to hunt the eighty acres on Saturday (the modern gun season would end on Sunday, November 21, 2018). I readily agreed because it is so nice to have someone to hunt with me in my old age, and he always knows where we should hunt. His big four-wheeler enclosed Rhino was out of commission due to need of a new transmission, so we took my 350 Yamaha four-wheeler. We had hunted that morning without killing a deer. Now, I don't think I have told you that he will not shoot a doe and he will not shoot a buck unless it has at least an eighteen-inch outside spread. It has to be a mighty good buck if he pulls the trigger. He also has not had a corn feeder on this eighty acre land this season.

After the morning hunt, without killing a deer, we decided we would drive to Arkadelphia (about ten miles) to get boxes of Kentucky Fried Chicken and drinks and head back to the lease where the little camp house sits. We ate pretty hurriedly sitting on plastic buckets, turned upside down, outside the little camp. When we finished our lunch, we decided to move one of his sixteen-foot metal stands to the place I had hunted that morning because he knew I really didn't like to hunt on the ground with a rotating stool against a tree, as I had done that morning. It was now about 3:00 p.m. After he moved the stand to the same location I was hunting in the morning, he went on to his stand about a mile away on another four-wheeler road. Now, I may have pointed this out earlier, but although it was a modern gun season, and I could have taken my 30-06 rifle, I decided I would take my Wolf Muzzleloader instead because (remember you can always hunt with a lesser weapon) I had already killed a doe with the modern gun and a small buck with the bow. Anyway, I got on that sixteen-foot metal stand and felt I was in hog heaven (excuse the pun) because there are many hogs on that land. About five fifteen, I saw this humongous buck easing down the trail eating acorns, and I knew he was coming right past my stand because I had on that great ScentLok suit and he could not smell me, so I cocked the gun. He paid no attention to me, and when he went right past a small tree not more than twenty feet from me and came back into an opening, I pulled the trigger. I knew that was a dead deer, but as you know, from my early remarks, the black powder smoke from the muzzleloader was very thick for a moment, and when it cleared, instead of seeing a dead deer right in front of my stand, I still could not see the dead monster buck, even with my small binoculars, as I had expected. My hunting buddy was probably hunting about a mile from me, but I knew he heard the shot and that he would also hunt until black dark (we always did). He heard the shot and sent me a fast text message on my cell phone asking if I had meat on the ground, and I said, "I think so." He said he would hunt until dark, and I knew he would. He had the four-wheeler.

I had just gotten down from my stand, and dark was fast approaching. As I started down that trail the deer was on, I saw a massive amount of blood, and I knew I would see a dead deer soon. Surely enough, I found him stone dead about fifty yards from my stand. I called my buddy who had not left his stand, but by now, it was getting really dark. Very soon, I heard my four-wheeler coming. I was sitting on a log guarding my prize. As soon as my young (now forty-six years old hunting buddy) got there, he hooked a piece of very strong mule rope around the deer's antlers. He had given me this exceptionally strong rope last year to put in my bag on front of my machine for such an occasion. We dragged that big buck behind the four-wheeler to the camp. I am sure it would have been a humorous sight to see that little 350 Yamaha four-wheeler carrying a 200# man, who was driving, a 140# woman behind him, and a humongous deer dragging behind up the hill to the camp.

The farther north one goes, the bigger the white tail deer get, so if you don't consider these "wall hangers" to be very large, you have to consider the southern state in which they were killed.

At eighty-six years old, I may not be able to hunt alone next season, but I have been blessed with good health so far, and whether I am blessed enough to hunt next year, I don't know, but I can tell you one thing, and that is what I have said and known through all the years I have hunted. There is nothing like good buddies, good friends, and a good deer hunt.

I had thought I might not have this last deer head mounted because I thought I would probably not live long enough to enjoy it many years, but immediately my friend A stepped up to the plate, just as my dad did with the 1990 (twelve-point buck). That friend said, "That is such a good deer that I am going to pay to have it mounted." This friend has never been on a deer hunt with me or anyone else. So perhaps I should have named this book *Good Buddies and Friends*, since I have enjoyed hunting so much from the cradle to the grave with good buddies and friends.

SUMMARY

If you should decide you will be, or already are, a good ethical deer hunter, my suggestion is to have good buddies, good friends, good deer equipment, and a love of nature. These things will make you a successful hunter and make your world go around no matter your age or sex.

Incidentally, I told you there would be a surprise at the end of this book. *I am an eighty-six year old female hunter, and buddies number one and number two were also females.*

So whether you are young or old, male or female, get going with the best sport you will ever experience from the cradle to the grave. I hope you have enjoyed the pictures which we took over the years so we would always have great memories of a lifetime of wonderful experiences. Incidentally, my little hunting buddy (number 2) took almost all the photos.

A B O U T   T H E   A U T H O R

Growing up in the Mississippi River Delta, I have enjoyed many kinds of hunting and fishing all my life, but deer hunting always appealed to me more than any other sport. I hunted almost from the cradle to the grave. I also played every sport available to me. I lived in the country where there was not much excitement and entertainment, but when the deer seasons opened, I could hardly wait. I learned to hunt with bow, shotgun, and rifle. My education consisted of a BS, MS, and PhD in biology, and I taught six years in high schools in Mississippi and Arkansas and thirty years in Arkadelphia, Arkansas, at Henderson State University, serving as teacher and chair of the biology department. I have also been a member of and authored and published more than forty scientific manuscripts in state and national journals. I have written biology lab manuals, authored religious books, and also poetry. I have been listed in over a dozen *Who's Who* books. I am a dedicated hunter, fisherman, and philosopher and will still be hunting until my grave.

www.ingramcontent.com/pod-product-compliance
Lightning Source LLC
Chambersburg PA
CBHW041107280526
45792CB00010B/2334